T0051144

BOOK OF BEGINNING HORN SOLOS

Edited by **David Ohanian**
of The Canadian Brass

■

All Selections Performed by
David Ohanian on horn,
and pianist Patrick Hansen

■

Plus Piano Accompaniments Only

Arranged by Bill Boyd

CONTENTS

The instrument pictured on the cover is a CB40 French Horn from The Canadian Brass Collection,
a line of professional brass instruments marketed by The Canadian Brass.

Photo: Gordon Janowiak

To access companion recorded performances
and accompaniments, visit:
www.halleonard.com/mylibrary

Enter Code
2547-8618-5632-5329

ISBN 978-0-7935-7246-5

Copyright © 1992 by HAL LEONARD
International Copyright Secured All Rights Reserved

www.canadianbrass.com
www.halleonard.com

World headquarters, contact:
Hal Leonard
7777 West Bluemound Road
Milwaukee, WI 53213
Email: info@halleonard.com

In Europe, contact:
Hal Leonard Europe Limited
42 Wigmore Street
Marylebone, London, W1U 2RN
Email: info@halleonardeurope.com

In Australia, contact:
Hal Leonard Australia Pty. Ltd.
4 Lentara Court
Cheltenham, Victoria, 3192 Australia
Email: info@halleonard.com.au

Dear Fellow Brass Player:

We might be just a little biased, but we believe that playing a brass instrument is one of the most positive activities that anyone can pursue. Whether you're 8 years old or 60 years old, the ability to play a horn automatically creates opportunities of playing with other people in bands, orchestras and ensembles throughout your life. But to keep yourself in shape and to better your playing, it's important to regularly work at solos. You might perform a contest solo for school, or play for a church service, or just for your family in the living room. Here's a book full of solos, in varied styles, that we think you'll enjoy learning.

All this music has been recorded for you on the companion audio. The Canadian Brass has recorded all the pieces in this collection on our respective instruments, letting you hear how the music sounds. Also you will find piano accompaniments for you to use in your practice, or if you wish, to perform with. The recordings of the solos that we have made should be used only as a guide in studying a piece. We certainly didn't go into these recording sessions with the idea of trying to create any kind of "definitive performances" of this music. There is no such thing as a definitive performance anyway. Each musician, being a unique individual, will naturally always come up with a slightly different rendition of a piece of music. We often find that students are timid about revealing their own ideas and personalities when going beyond the notes on the page in making music. After you've practiced for weeks on a piece of music, and have mastered all the technical requirements, you certainly have earned the right to play it in the way you think it sounds best! It may not be the way your friend would play it, or the way The Canadian Brass would play it. But you will have made the music your own, and that's what counts.

Good luck and Happy Brass Playing!
The Canadian Brass

DAVID OHANIAN came to The Canadian Brass with a rich and varied musical background. Born to musician parents, the highlight of his earlier musical studies came at Fountainbleu, France, where at age sixteen he won a scholarship to study with Nadia Boulanger. He earned a degree from the New England Conservatory of Music, after which, at the age of twenty-four, he found himself in the unlikely predicament of simultaneously being offered horn positions with two of the world's great orchestras, the Chicago and Boston Symphonies. He joined the Boston Symphony and played there for eleven years, and also with the Boston Pops under Arthur Fiedler. As a founding member of the Empire Brass, David left orchestral playing in 1981 devote his full time to that quintet's career. When the horn position became open in The Canadian Brass in 1986, David's experience in quintet playing, his broad knowledge of repertory, and his flair for performing made him the natural choice for the group.

PATRICK HANSEN, pianist, has been musical coach and assistant conductor at Des Moines Metro Opera, and has served on the staff of Juilliard Opera Center as a coach and accompanist. He was assistant editor on the new G. Schirmer Opera Anthology, and has recorded several other albums for Hal Leonard. Patrick holds degrees in piano from Simpson College and the University of Missouri at Kansas City.

CANADIAN BRASS BLUES

Bill Boyd

YANKEE DOODLE

Traditional American

STREETS OF LAREDO

American Folksong (adapted from old Irish air)

ODE TO JOY

Adapted from Symphony No. 9
by Ludwig van Beethoven

AMERICA

Words by Samuel F. Smith
Music by Henry Carey

CARNIVAL OF VENICE

Julius Benedict

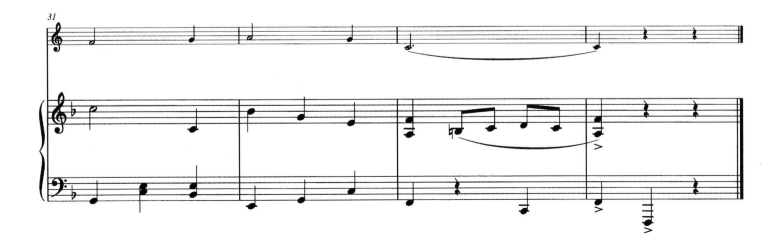

THE RIDDLE SONG

English ballad

FINLANDIA

Jean Sibelius

CANADIAN BRASS BLUES

FRENCH HORN

Bill Boyd

YANKEE DOODLE

Traditional American

2

STREETS OF LAREDO

American Folksong (adapted from old Irish air)

ODE TO JOY

Adapted from Symphony No. 9
by Ludwig van Beethoven

AMERICA

Words by Samuel F. Smith
Music by Henry Carey

CARNIVAL OF VENICE

Julius Benedict

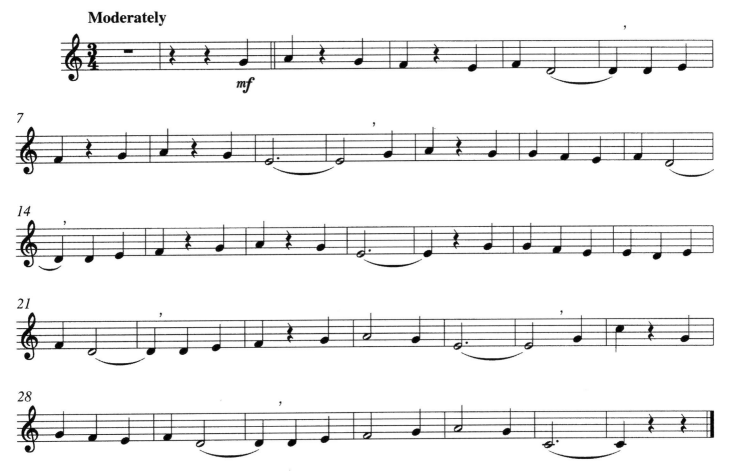

4

THE RIDDLE SONG

English ballad

Moderately

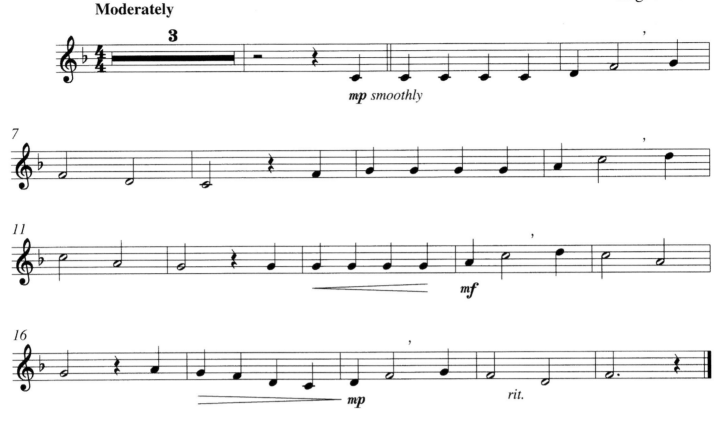

mp smoothly

mf

mp
rit.

FINLANDIA

Jean Sibelius

Moderately

mp legato

mf

mp

AMAZING GRACE

Words by John Newton
Traditional American melody

THE SKATERS

Emil Wauldteufel

6

MARINE'S HYMN

Words by unknown marine (1847)
Music by Jacques Offenbach

TAKE ME OUT TO THE BALL GAME

Words by Jack Norworth
Music by Albert von Tilzer

7

SONG OF THE VOLGA BOATMAN

Russian Folksong

THE CRUEL WAR IS RAGING

American Folksong

DOXOLOGY

Words by Thomas Ken
Music by Louis Bourgéois

GIVE MY REGARDS TO BROADWAY

Words and Music by George M. Cohan

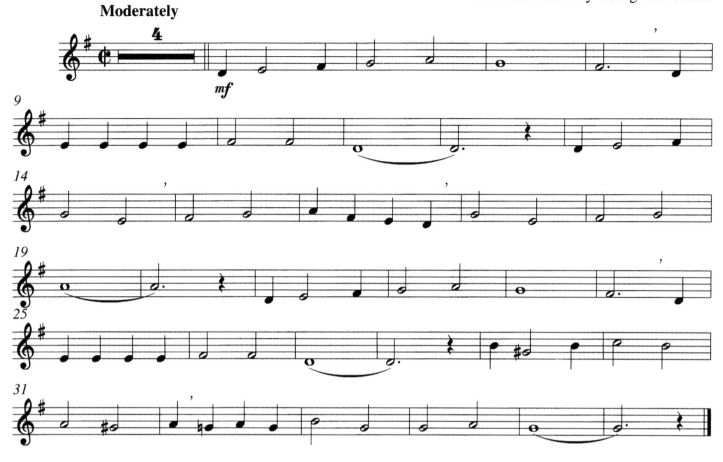

JUST A CLOSER WALK

Words and Music by Red Foley

AMAZING GRACE

Words by John Newton
Traditional American melody

THE SKATERS

Emil Wauldteufel

MARINE'S HYMN

Words by unknown marine (1847)
Music by Jacques Offenbach

TAKE ME OUT TO THE BALL GAME

Words by Jack Norworth
Music by Albert von Tilzer

SONG OF THE VOLGA BOATMAN

Russian Folksong

THE CRUEL WAR IS RAGING

American Folksong

DOXOLOGY

Words by Thomas Ken
Music by Louis Bourgéois

GIVE MY REGARDS TO BROADWAY

Words and Music by George M. Cohan

JUST A CLOSER WALK

Words and Music by Red Foley